T0100262

NATIONAL ANIMAL

National Animal

DEREK WEBSTER

THE POETRY IMPRINT AT VÉHICULE PRESS

Published with the generous assistance of the Canada Council for the Arts, the Canada Book Fund of the Department of Canadian Heritage, and the Société de développement des entreprises culturelles du Québec (SODEC).

Signal Editions editor: Carmine Starnino
Cover design: David Drummond
Typeset in Minion and Filosofia by Simon Garamond
Printed by Livres Rapido Books

Library and Archives Canada Cataloguing in Publication

Title: National animal / Derek Webster.
Names: Webster, Derek (Poet), author.
Description: Poems.
Identifiers: Canadiana (print) 20240322096 | Canadiana (ebook) 2024032210X | ISBN 9781550656572 (softcover) | ISBN 9781550656619 (EPUB)
Subjects: LCGFT: Poetry.
Classification: LCC PS8645.E254 N38 2024 | DDC C811/.6—dc23

Published by Véhicule Press, Montréal, Québec, Canada

Distribution in Canada by LitDistCo
www.litdistco.ca

Distribution in US by Independent Publishers Group
www.ipgbook.com

Printed in Canada

For
Saleema,
Vivienne, and Larkin

In memory of my father
Norman Webster,
and friend
Marina Havadejova

Contents

ALUMINUM SADNESS

THE THINKER

King Canute

We are debating the limits of power
one night late at the kitchen table.
"Canute told his soldiers to attack the waves,"
says my father –
                "and there his reign ended,"
I cut in, "but for the crying."

He looks surprised. I am thirty-one, tired
of the wise king's lessons. He sighs.
The king was trying to say something.

In the glass door's reflection, our deaf-mute alternates
swing mythic objects, stabbing
at what they fear in the dark.
                      Outside
by a gopher's den, furred shoulders shiver
and crows blink their third lids. Under grass
water marches, slaughtering the hills.

IMPERIAL SILENCE

The Writing on the Wall

The graffiti eraser in Montreal
blasts the red brick wall with water,
removing *Vive le Québec libre.*

Earlier this week he scrubbed off *fugg it*
and *baise-moi*, stencils of tanks and skulls,
a few fat dicks, one *whore*, sixteen illegible tags,

three *anglo go home* and a dozen *amour.*
He applies milky soap to one-eyed feelings,
the mad skilz and torqued hate

learned in school or bar. Sprayed again,
the wall explodes into pictures:
a palm tree in a Lotto Max sky –

Bob Marley's smiling, dreadlocked head –
fireworks on *la fête nationale* –
something to fear. The generator cuts

and a secular silence fills the civic moment.
Slicker open, the man smokes by his van
as toxins leach from the wall

and the fading words almost disappear.
But what does it matter? They will return.
A thing notwithstanding is always there.

National Animal

Amid mud-hardened branches, it hates
whatever once kept it greasy and warm,
its formaldehydean psyche, half-duck,
adrift in this foreign home.

It chews up the book
of what it was – finds
on the next page, enraged,
its story keeps going.

This is Jerusalem the crowned lady
on the wall smiles. Winter
or summer, it trembles, gnawing
on itself, surviving on its wiles.

Portrait with Stuffed Jackalope

Something like divine justice afflicts us.
Look at the signs: bushes light themselves ablaze,
icebergs run as lemmings into overcrowded seas,
squid-like plastic bags hang from branches.
Remember when the great rivers raced backwards
and trees, bodies, houses, hills were driven under?
Now the lucky unlucky pierce our perimeter,
starving, against their older judgement.

You used to say *It's not too late* before praying
mantises climbed the sugar-water dispenser
and garrotted the hummingbirds. I painted you
as Francis Bacon would, had he been painting
a predatory beauty just coming to life, eating
through the skull of an old, iridescent hope.

Video of a Cougar, YouTube

She swats the air in front of him, forepaws wide,
wants to lop off his head and lope off to hide
her cubs trotting behind her down the rocky trail.
No! No! he gasps, tripping backward, arms raised.
Scarlet, orange, and pink in the viral trees.
I am watching the vicarious thrill of his fear
grow dull. *Stop stalling and pounce already.*
But I know he'll survive. He pleads for donations

to preserve wildlife habitat, stop the grass lawns
moving up the hillside. I can't take this anymore.
"Our long national nightmare is over" the next
clip proclaims. In my sleep, her prowling tongue
laps up permethrin, then diazinon, condensed
in the saddle of a mountain lake, riding the fog.

Ghost Bike

The moment flipped. I knew I'd die. I flew
over his truck's red hood. Into the ground
I went, my people crying all around.
If only they could see themselves, the view
beyond their streets and jobs and untied laces.
I do not hate him. Here, we do not love.
It is a gift. Like removing a glove
to find pure light instead of hand. No faces
swooning, no pigeons hunched along the wires
mimicking notes on staves. No heavenly choirs.
I wheeled and spun, cherished my tiny load
as the wind brushed my cheek. All that dull length
I fought to stay. Then breathing out, found strength
to rise, and let me die, there in the road.

Burning Building

Look: through clouds as brown as earth, whiffs
of moth balls and dried-up rat turds, a neon flash
of legs, glinting picks, then banded arms
and swinging elephant nozzles emerge.
The firemen. They crack windows like break-in experts:
knock out the bottom first, raise the axe's thick side
to the pane, then tap the top till the whole piece
slips without sound from its frame.

One tells me, smiling, "Smoke's the air we breathe."
The pink ungoggled socket-eyed faces!
They laugh and talk, shoulder their tanks, slip
their masks back on, rub the sooty trenches
from their necks. Entering the choked mouth again,
through bursting smoke their crowbars sing.

Blanche Dubois at Mercy Asylum

The Sisters of Mercy welcome all all
get carded hosed fingerprinted clothed
injected tested x-rayed spinal tapped
sedated that's when the screaming stops
and they sit alone in the common room
until Herr Doktor invites them to his room
observing the folds of their total personality
then Jimmy presents abstract art says give
each picture a title sets patients to drawing
masterpieces in pencil and it's dinnertime
after fifteen days some just sit in the library
some go home some knit and unknit sweaters
no grandson would ever wear some loudly pray
in the chapel with voices dumb or penitent
upward stares and some scribble the Great
American Novel in secret from which the next
day in the trash nothing may be obtained

The days unspool at the sewing machine
in the kitchen the garden the latrines we are
either on duty or old biddies rocking in chairs
rest rest all we do here must have meaning
some days I jaw till my jaw goes slack
on Saturdays they project a film on the wall
where the valiant maiden gets tied to the rails
or voodoo witchdoctors in a cave blow smoke
up her thighs got to rein in that wandering uterus
and if that don't work there's always trepanation
but she only collapses never quite dies someone

saves her in time for her cold wet sheet pack
administered to those with hypermotor conditions
yes really it's quite hysterical –

There's the main wing for the men and another
houses all the backward children and we castoffs
at the back in a stubby protrusion my window
abuts the field where an old chap cuts the grass
and paints white lines and beyond that vast expanses
of swamp to Metarie Ridge *quelle vue* through the
bars I watch rats make war on the strays and at
twilight cover my ears when I hear them coming
the men with rifles leading boys into the midden
there are some scenes you don't want replayed

Balance is my problem the lack makes me
unhealthy in Laurel they tied the crazies to trees,
children threw stones at them strangers sought predictions
who'll win the big game will it rain tomorrow
is the market going to crash again they asked
oh those poor Pollyannas chained to quercus virginiana
though not my old cousins with delirium tremens
they took long walks in the park held up by a servant
cuckoos circling their papery temples they were
house-poor and mad but never disrespected
it runs in the family yes membership has privileges

Since coming here I have stabilized certainly
the electroshock treatments help me greatly
though one never stops feeling everything
there is comfort in being sad thinking of Stella
slapping the brute likely as not she has
another baby and subscribes to Life magazine

whenever Papa whipped her she'd say *Blanche
I deserved it* yes there's relief in comeuppance
sitting potato-like discussing one's problems
but I won't forgive our father or that anytown
he dropped us into home is where they hate you
so I can't go home no I can't go home

Night-times in the hall the mop echoes *slip slop*
and the janitor whistles as he works and I hear
him shout up the balcony stairs and see him
swagger in drunk again his snake eyes on me
and all his whispered cruelties run me through
my emotions like a racehorse on amphetamines

I tried to escape this oilcloth reality furnished
myself with perfumed vials instead of black bile
and yellow bile and phlegmatic colonels oh
Asclepius heal me do I have a cock for you
sterilization is one route to prevent Christine
Jorgensens but Edna's voice was always high
and sweet as a schoolboy's so far as I know
they put her to sleep and took her down
to the theatre and spread her legs for a muckle
of medical students and off came her privates

Mostly my fellow required guests are
poor loners or rejected mothers none can
find a use for anymore years of noisy silence
a grim-faced background disturbance like Jenny
raking sad patches of soil so long nothing grows
or the hotbox on days she's flushed and agitated
she flung a diaperful of blood at Sister Greta
and there are others the Air National Guard

girl who can't stop scratching and Roberta
the farmwife with no teeth she grips
the metal fence as if the world were a tilt-
a-whirl and she holding on for dear life
till Marcus rings the bell time to come in lunch-
time Roberta they have to pry her fingers off
and she can't work in the laundry or the kitchen
and she gets all wide-eyed at the sight of a sink
prefers cool under the cedars no noise

Today I pleaded Herr Doktor when can
I make a new start *Well Miss Dubois* he says
Do you think you are ready and I say Well yes
when I came here I was sick and so angry
and full of delusions about Stanley but I
have lived and learned and grown here I'd
like to return to my old hometown yes
they'll sneer and stare but you've given
me a life I never thought I'd have and
it's all been so wonderful

and he smiles and polishes his spectacles
I can tell he likes me yes I am his pet
lizard on a string but I don't eat flies
no I don't do that and he asks *What
is your feeling, Miss Dubois, about lobotomy?*
and I say I know nothing of these medical
miracles but I hear good only good things
of lobotomy Herr Doktor – *Just doctor* he says
*There is also lithium, it's new, a bit radical, but I feel
for you the former may prove more successful*
and a slit of light down the hall opens and
slams and I understand without treatment
he will never let me leave

It is silent inside the hospital the wind
carries sounds from the street young lovers
laughing and a man with a guitar strolling
a knock unanswered *corones para los muertos*
I wish Stella would write or visit or send
pictures of her babies how many two three
no eight yes eight years at the mercy of Mercy
Stella knows I would never lie about that
yet his word still holds me down remember
the martyrs had to burn through disbelief for their
ideals to twist to truths but my own sister
even she doesn't believe me

I was not ready for what could be who could
slapped then dragged by the hair on my knees
to the marriage bed how could one bear
thinking on it so forcibly until it was done
in a corner a leather ball stitches pulled out
he goes into the parlour to drink while
slowly I limp off to clean myself that night
a bright torch glowing Vulcan still hammering
his ugly face grinning for Aphrodite a gift
she did not want but must accept dawn
in her hole looking upward pale pink light
made to be admired the men bowed to her
why did she pick the loathsome one control
why couldn't I stop him

They're building highways out my window
the dynamite thunders another house falls
into a small cloud of dust and Fords and Bel
Airs and other giant finned cars soon they'll
swim their way across Lake Pontchartrain
and Eisenhower will be up for reelection

The nurses smile and stare down
for my own safety the straps stop me
floating out the window they turn to him
he shows me the pick says when I awaken
I'll be reborn a new woman plagued
no more by thoughts akin to locusts
I believe him I want to leave this place I
I am Sleeping Beauty groggy on my gurney
the brute had his way yes but my sister
committed me to the kindness of strangers

Double Dream of Joni Mitchell

"I drew a map of Canada…
with your face sketched on it twice"

She's holding an orange prairie lily
across from the Bess in Saskatoon,
provoking again the forty-ninth question.
Flip me over – who would I be
on the other side? On stepped-down
winter trails, to the bar, where you'll turn
the facets on your tumbler of salted beer
as Mary Hart's legs light up the grainy satellite.
That's how the great comparison begins.

Up in Laurel Canyon, aluminum sadness,
the faun on the runway and walls of sound.
She remembers home, riding a sweet bicycle
under those high white palaces at twilight.
Feels, like Neil, all her changes were there.
With slim strumming fingers she picks
up her pen, fills the hot shape of emptiness.
A song for both sides now.

Dresden

As Mahler's Fourth drones through the air
I think of my grandfather down on one knee
in blue overalls, tools beside him on the floor
behind the ancient refrigerator.

He would cough and shift, and soon leave
events like this, a tuxedo fundraiser
more social than beneficial,
his mind ungrounded, still in the war.

So much still needs fixing.
I see the grand chandelier
falling. Bass, kettle, truthful drum.
Even the bomb-jaded must have known

the tone was wrong, each ear listening
as the overture clattered and hummed
for three days, more than two thousand planes
bursting through the walls of their homes.

In my velour chair, I remember the country boys
my grandfather trained to fly at Centralia
and Summerside, PEI. I see them turning,
pulling the lever of the bomb-bay doors,

feel the knife of cold air at their throats
as the tonnage whistles in darkness dropping
upon a million civilians and refugees,
their eyes glowing red crystals

reflecting the firestorm
igniting all around them,
the wet surfaces of their tongues
melting with unvoiced lessons.

Outside the concert hall, I look up:
ashes and shadow-entities are falling,
white thoughts with small parachutes
trumpeting their own burials.

Step Up, Step Up

Ten thousand oxen drag the Ark to water.
Munching on the last two Karner Blue butterflies,
the escaped orangutans note the broken power lines
and beige skidmark of the keel.

Two straws from a latte, the giraffes give a silent hum
as yellow truncheons rain down on a stowaway
family of gophers. Worker bees
dance prophetic Jeremiads

and shed their wings before dying
upside-down in a humid pile,
and the hammered resolve of the Pasha's elephants
trumps the brown ocean's rising, eggy tide.

Finally, the waters are rising! The mountains
move closer, their snowless peaks now bleached with guano.
Clark Gables, Lionel Messis, Vladimir Putins, Marie Antoinettes:
all want a second helipad in the bow.

Toasting the faith of wolves, they refresh their platinum tablets.
It's a charging bull market. Who needs an oar?
Step up, step up and place your bets
on how long the albatross will soar.

Dominion

1.

At the cabin door
           spring wavers.
Undressing, sighing –

seal mitts
      great coat
               beaver hat

a gaunt figure
      unwound, the tartan scarf
          revealing a face –

II.

Birch creak and deer bark and
                    other alarums.

They come
                    wrapped in rabbit hoods
with spears.
                    Others
come wrapped
                    in sheep's wool
and Christian fervor.

In their ordinary desperation
                    they know why
not what
                    they are accepting –

III.

Were you welcomed at the gate by Elders?
How was your seat?
What of the windows of your soul?

Were you given a choice
of language and/or beverage?
English, French, soft pretzels, Cree?

From your prolonged exposure
to Canada, would you recommend it
for headaches? coughing, sneezing, dry throat?

Clickety go the rails, *clack* go the keys.

IV.

A crowd gathers. I deny knowing
this place.
Don Cherry crows three times.

When the ice melts, Canada & I
re-emerge, arms locked like wrestlers
in frozen embrace. *The Mail and Empire:*

TWO BODIES FOUND IN ALLEY

"Their faces are so familiar"
says a bystander. "Yet I can't say
I truly recognize either."

v.

Our canoe keeps sinking.
Something inside remains too heavy,
flowing in and out when seasons change,
escaping all our frantic bailing.

Who stands vigilant on the shore?
What animal calls from the ripening wheat?

VI.

Drive by your old life –
       the hills produce shadows
       the future buries

and the birds sing oblivion
       estranged from all things

as you follow an Abenaki trail
       through ghostly thin-rumped horses

past the grey-green, half-forgotten monuments
       mottled by pigeons
       imperial in their silence

VII.

Northern fields
                    depend upon
blackened snow
          the mud glistening
with ice   meltwater

beside a fawn's
                    skeleton

VIII.

Looking out the window
I catch my higher self
smiling in the street below.

I shout *Hey!* then hurry
down to meet –
but he is gone.

I am still waiting, here
on my window ledge, waving
my government money

as the radio speaks of rain.
I think of my friends
and miss many.

IX.

Dove-grey on blue, a canoe turns
back over. Maple syrup, jam, a rubber sheet
bobbing underneath. Across the coloured quilt

of lakes, a breeze
floats down down
the cliff's cooling face.

Tom Thompson,
let my quiet art
contain your true weather.

x.

Between the highway's cut faces
of rock, my mother sings along
to saccharine songs, looking back
over the car seat, now and then
smiling down –
                        Miss Canada
knows how to draw a protest
                        a grudging laugh
from little me
            and in that moment
                            a grain slips
            inside the heart's cage –
                        starts to itch
to lacquer itself
            and as a compromise
produces beauty.

XI.

Let the spell of unspoken
                              be broken.
Let the spoken be acted upon.

Rightness cannot be inherited.
If you want it
                    you must
obtain it by great labor.

Dominion   help us
                            love you
for new reasons.

MISS CANADA

The Boy's Own Annual, 1879-1967

Biggles lends us his shiny machete
and pith helmet moldy with jungle rain.
Rapt at bedtime, we lie awake rehearsing
his machine-gun lesson to the Zulus,
swoon for the lilywhite orphans he burns
from their teepees, raised by the Sioux.
Civilization is a wizened forearm
holding a plate of cucumber sandwiches.

Our manservant Semper Fidelis – a prince
of Bengal before losing to us – puts out the light.
In dreams we untie Mother from the rails
and grind Lothario's mustache under heel.
We've all the advice a million boys could hope for
on which of the lesser nations to conquer.

An Old Painting of Charleston Harbor

Did the man and the boy, foreground, in hats,
walk out on the Lord's Day and down to the shore
after the sun had passed over the indigo?

As they talk in the clean salt air, are they
recalling home, chasing off the scent of danger
that comes through the dark at the calling hour?

Are they humming lullabies the man's mother sang,
singing words about happy and ruinous things
feeling the same? Or should we listen

to words unsaid – how bodies at first smell sweet
when they rot, or how, if one peered through holes in a hull
the waves could seem like rolling hills,

and a vile captain's voice might caress and trill
before setting an example. Or how pantless sailors
squatting over gunwales might say "We'll be there soon"

for forty days and nights – and when they reached
these much-contested waters, and the hold was opened,
the man and boy were the only cargo left alive.

Stop.
       This is canvas layered with colours.
This man, this boy, are framing agents
       placed there
               to create depth

to make the bay appear
        more picturesque –

                shapely stand-ins

for anticipated viewers
                who may look (or may not)
        like you and I – and in truth

it is difficult to discern
        whether that is dark coat
                or bare arm.

After two hundred years, if
                these deft shapes – head
thrown back,

arm raised – seem to cry
                out from the shore
of their captured world,

who hears them? Reader, as you
        remake the prospect
of Charleston Harbor,

what do *you* see
        in that empty spot
on the water?

Meditation on a Puzzle

If you stopped, mid-reconstruction, you'd recall
doing this jigsaw two decades ago. How could you forget
the fist bursting from soil, or the cemetery at night
with its dozen shades of brown? But finishing it
didn't make you whole. Its purpose was distraction.
When you find the missing loop of the water tower,
notice orange light a hundred feet above the killing floor,
as always, the mayor's apologies have come too late.

The motel's angry neon has switched on. What you
remember as a brandy bottle is actually a beating heart.
The picture didn't change, you did. You have left the ranks
of wishful reconstituters. Alone in your walnut
library, sun falling behind the gathering crowds,
a dire new task presents itself.

Naught

The three boys stand with sticks near dawn
raiding the empty manse, their snow-white tracks
lighting the blackened lawn.

Already from the char of timber stacks
they've claimed a gold-tipped drill,
a jewelry chest, a scorched-brown axe,

the three-legged charcoal grill.
A cast-iron pan lies steaming off the dew.
Last night they'd seen smoke on the hill

and after milking, through the wood-doves' coo
they'd walked as one to catch the end.
Out here, there's naught to do

but wait till God's will cools, then rend
a use from what can't last.
Out here, only wet-eyed strangers defend

an absent laird or mourn the looted past.
Save your pity for worlds to come:
bored boys go nowhere fast

until it's their time to get some.
Then fee. Then fie. Then foe. Then fum.

Yearlings

No longer mottled, driven off,
the yearling makes a new path through forest
going left, going right, snorting at
nosed branches which invite
its body
— we will forever
be finding our own ways to it —

around
a stubborn, wet stump
across the white flowering bog, the scattered bones,
back to its grazing art, each spring
a tired, brown line.

Born to green, yearlings
startle
themselves
to a musky vim,
creaturely sound, unseen
emerging from the crackling canopy
or passing unheard
— and bow heads
and kick alive —
and gone.

Ancient, unnamed,
a humid bubble
leaves our mouths, wants to stay
among the top-heavy bulrushes, glassed
with ice, leaning toward the road.

Study of a Dying Tree

Neon ants, lithe along its bulk,
buzz off chunks in the fatherless light.

From the unsupported canopy, things crawl out.
A shock to see what was always there.

The fence accordioned, its drunken slats
crushed by wooden music.

Post-lightning, on its knees,
elbows dug in the ground.

Halfway across the field, white forearms
puncture the skin of lawn.

A cloud of sawdust, hungry
and writhing, gathers above the lake.

Kitsune

The fox hesitates
at glassy presences,
at this sombre angle
retreats, cocks
his hungry head
at cyanide morsels.
Am I here? A high
cyclopean being
answers the soft
question, flexing
itself alive
as the new door

hardens to a mirror
and an image runs
off reversed

he leans into it
the old heaviness
slides open
with a whoosh –
over eggshells
he takes a cold
shape, voiceless
whistle landing
in folds of inner
ear. Dawn pushes
outward. Shift
workers wake.

Night Thought

for Steven Heighton

There's no plan for growing into a body.
A fire burns itself across your field
and when it has passed, you remain, a still thing
hairless in charred grass and earthen wind,
gasping at the wrap of bare arms.

Nor is there any plan for growing into a country.

Lying here, next to snoring Miss Canada
I no longer hear blood's machine gun
propagate in my ears. Outside, on the river,
a mirrored concept barely exists,
murky line of light waking in the saying.

In the Country

Shaggy bulls philosophize under yellow trees
while calves buck at a bent stick
as if it were a snake.
Walk to the shore of the lake.
Pick up a rock. Skip it.
Imagine, deep in woods, sleeping coyotes.

If you squeeze cotton balls into your ears,
the *thumb-thump* of cars on the bridge
and low hum of electric fencing
will fade to almost nothing.
The snake of our age
will sleep without a care.

Make your small sacrifice: a sense of gratitude,
a ground-up beech leaf,
a mental prayer.
August light, like honey in a jar,
drips with belief
the world does not seek to harm you.

Homemade Blueberry Wine

My friend, don't ask me to pretend
now you've made me drink this stuff
that it's "amazing," "wow," or even
"surprisingly good." Let's be honest:
your grog is a gut-punch to the kisser.

I never knew wine could be meaty, sour
and evocative of cake all at the same time.
Let's order a pizza, and pour your
shark piss into a large punchbowl.
It may still make a passable sangria.

And now we've downed the whole bowl –
laughing as we eat the alcohol-soaked
oranges and using the pizza crusts
like edible fishing rods – it's time to become
philosophers. No more complaining

about empty bank accounts, air-guitaring
on the coffee table, no whining about
the white-collar salt mines or how our
quiet, manly tears go unrecognized.
No! It's time to pardon the turkey.

Let's be honest: this is the greatest wine
known to man. I feel more virile than a
decorated veteran who's just won
Stanley with a game-seven, overtime,
out-of-his-jockstrap-goalie-deking goal.

Alright time to calm down or your
new dog's going to lose its other eye.
Stop the shouting and techno music,
my head feels like the Grinch's heart
crushed between two Whoville cymbals

and forgive the terrible things I whispered
in your ear during your spontaneous,
seven-minute coma. No one will love us
like we love ourselves tonight. Lionel
Richie said that. Or was it Whitney?

Piggery Road

Having sleepwalked to the iced creek
you awaken to squealing wind,
whiptails of snowdrifts, caged dogs barking

and wild boar tracking back, into
the living trellis of twigs and branches,
path of a carcass

                      dragged off the road by mouth.
You return to yourself
        barefoot along a thin gravel thread

        an unpaved I
that washes out each spring.
                  Limp, now

into the far hill's shadows,
back to those pink ghosts, fifty-million strong
who gave this road a name.

Up there, someplace, is my home.

ALUMINUM SADNESS

Birdstrike

I turn it in my hand,
in the morning,
a stunned thing

wonder of ivory
hooks, iridescent
feathered skin.

What was that
green, invisible,
what was lost

am I
night waiting
in its undercoat

Ravens

Painful, to be so close
to their stately, scared presence –

their language unknown
to me, they with

no consciousness
of me or mine, I

like most poets
like Klein

a continuation
of lake and pine.

Teenagers

We climb from the pool in the afternoon
and dry in the hot sun.

It is happening. We are becoming
harder versions of ourselves.

One among us takes off
her clothes.

We're all curled up
inside our skins, waiting

for the seams to rip,
new people to step out.

Tannery Hill

He climbed the drainpipe to her room. There
she confessed love for another. Her words
returned as he backed down unsound ladders,
house-painting in summer to clear his debts.

In small notes he apostrophized her name
as if sky and water ran within each letter
till she changed her mind on Tannery Hill,
her basket full of picnic necessities.

Then the now of who they were stopped fitting
the small terms of who they said they'd be.

Drying on a rack, his biking shorts
stared back at him, disconsolate
in basement shade among the pickle jars,
"Cruel Summer" on the radio upstairs.

At the golf course restaurant her father liked,
she told him, please, to join the tennis club.
He ate his penne vodka-sauce in silence
as the tint-glass sun went down on empty links.

Tannery Hill, a place to flay and cure skin
to make it change, force value from it again.
Tannery Hill, the place they once led cows
to slaughter, eased from pastures into town.

Walter Benjamin in Moscow

Walter Benjamin is girl crazy!
Follows Asja Lacis like a sad puppy
to the trolley doors, still detailing

the revolution's ideals.
"Did they fire into the crowd again?" he asks.
"All they wanted was bread!" she screams.

Be patient. He's written half of nothing.
"I miss the books in my library," he sighs.
"You should write about that," I say.

A theatrical friend, killed right beside her.
To raise spirits, Walt makes fondue.
"In truth," she sighs, "he was a terrible actor."

Time to go. I leave him a note:
It ends in Portbou. It ends in sleep.
Do not be afraid of these industrial times.

Apartment Block

The secretary's heels echo
as she climbs the concrete stairs.
Her door slams. Wheeled recycling bins
stand at attention, guard yellow walls.
Ants disassemble a strip of bulgogi beef.

The weight won't lift
from the glue-sniffers' shoulders. A pulse,
a dance beat: some kid turns up his stereo,
finds his rhythm: priests in heavy robes,
beatings, fiddle reels, oily tracks.

Down the hall, in a chair
held together by duct tape and
molded foam, a veteran dies.
A man in espadrilles looks up, surprised
by the knock at his door. Another month unpaid.

This building is a business
not a charity. Thrown out the windows,
tenants' belongings fill the courtyard,
settle on the bones of small animals
that also failed to thrive here.

Fletcher's Field

And now the lark and starling sing.
Now refraction comes through rain.
A child runs to find me across the playground
in Fletcher's Field.

If I climb this ladder, reach down
cavalier from the roof to paint the eaves –
if I fall, could I make
another life, grey streak in my hair?

All these years, I have lived as if a thought
could sink me like a paper boat
and have tried to trace back the creek
that carried me out to sea.

Marina

Wind pushed us up the long hill, toward
your family home, lodged in a crown of chestnut trees
and tendrilled ruins. My backpack bright with badges
sewn during long nights on trains and buses

clacking past sheep in County Galway,
spinach fields in Surrey, a cheese town in France,
children running alongside the moving windows,
toward the eastern reaches,

the sweet beers of Prague, neo-Nazi skinheads
in the subway at night, slowing to pass
Romany villages then onward
into Slovakia, to Presov, your home.

We hiked the Tatras, took refuge in goat-breaks
from passing storms, sang Ave Maria,
ate borsht in the shelter, cooled our baby-pink feet
in mountain streams.

When I'd returned to Canada, you crawled into the lap
of your aging mother. You drew the clouds over you
like sheets. The machine pumped air lungward.
How much more? "Soon," they said, "no more."

Marina, I would walk the ocean floor, cross Atlantic ridges
and trace the Rhine upstream to knock on your door.
To hear Joho on the banjo, Seki with his accordion,
and Katerina starting another song.

Oakville Revisited

In the wide mouth of the Sixteen-Mile Creek,
the spring ice has flowed and broken up.
Seagulls lope through the sky above as the hum
of town life drifts down to the shore.
There, figures walk slowly, holding hands
in black clothes, recalling the action of days
while thoughts from night's two edges remain
shadowed by the lighthouse at the end of the pier.
Yet this green-grey shore is still the same,

here where Navy Street climbs slightly to the old centre,
past tennis courts, and yachts, and welcoming homes
in need of paint, blue spruce and pine fronting their yards.
The streetlights shudder and treetops bend:
wind is sweeping overhead, busting off the lake,
arriving wild in Oakville, growing slow and tame.
By Church and Robinson it skirts downtown,
past the cafes, giftshops for kids and pet-food stores,
chocolate displays, and two boutiques for yarn,
with clean cement sidewalks and parklettes
bearing historical names on patches of green.

Behind the built-up facades, the lake stretches,
miles and miles of emerald grey, and sailboats'
white triangles look back on undercut, collapsing cliffs
and muscular, bulwarked seawalls. At night, lights
of Hamilton, highways and refineries, and eastward,
distant pinpricked beacons atop the CN Tower.
Leaving the valley of the Sixteen-Mile, cars roll
on their way to ramps and malls and timely GO trains,

through the haze of warehouses and depots along the Q-E
to the white boxes of Ford on a hill, and beyond,
Winston Churchill Boulevard. All this time,
winter or summer, the lake-water gleams,
white stars on grey and blue, calling to sailors
and ghosts of deer, leaping on Tannery Hill.

Often at full moon, the teenagers
gather to smoke under the bridge, satirical trolls
making fun of their world: *Jokeville, No Hopeville.*
Sons of investment bankers, daughters of physicians,
they're embarrassed to admit the opposite, that the town
was set up to win, by years of good stewardship, wealth
and location. Before dawn, the teens long gone,
small owls make their final run, picking off mice
venturing to the riverside for snacks of chrysalides.

The wind picks up. Columns of air kilometres high
heat the high atmosphere, spilling coldness down
as the sun hits Lakeshore Road, toothing morning.
The pizza joint sits dusty and still. In the yoga gym
with tinted windows, the stale sweat stirs. In the lot
of gravestones and monuments, the sparrows gather
as delivery of fish and bread in the alleys begins.
Through little holes in walls, oubliettes in the walk,
the slam of trays and smells of cooking come.
In the frozen-yogourt shop just past the core,
a franchise owner in a lopsided swivel chair
assesses her prospects beside industrial refrigerators

while, glancing up from flowerbeds, a crew of workers
nods to another in a passing streetsweeper.
An acrid taste hits the tongue: roofers burn acetylene

as a saw whines, two tones, catching wood again
and again. The private schools will open, but not today,
today the creek is full of paddlers, the dangle
of Olympic gold just beyond their straining necks.
On the bank, an old lady and her terrier stop to watch
the smooth crews parting the liquid calm.
Retirees with bad knees in ragged dressing gowns
bend to pick up papers tossed by cycling newsboys
as coffee thunders quietly and toast pops, indoors.

Church bells will ring, but not yet. Two bleary drinkers
must wake in their car, where they bundled up
after last call, grew sick, and passed out in the cold.
I remember it all, I tell myself. Fake IDs, Brewer's Retail,
orange juice and vodka, Aerosmith on the jukebox,
the man at the Murray House who fell from the roof.
In the library, the empty reading chairs glow, ignoring all,
while the smiling faces of actors in this season's plays
stare out crazily from posters in the theatre foyer.
If one looked up now, a hawk would be there, circling,
hoping to catch a starling hissing a raspberry, unawares,
as a boy holds his mother's hand inside the bank,
and words mumbled, under the breath, of withdrawals –
a cavernous, single room, the only sound a ticking clock.

Private-School Survey

The survey arrives with smiling student pictures:
no gravy stains on blazers, no whipped-red asses,
no sleeping mouths a-drool on sports-tournament buses.
How would you like your newsletter, virtual or paper?
Ah, the math problem of self: If your body is a train
travelling forward, who sees what has passed?
But I still like the clap of chapel bells, even as
I know their promise to protect rings hollow.

Judgement was everywhere. On Good Friday. On the ice.
In our second-guessed hearts. In low whispers
when someone didn't play their part. The tide turned, that
world receded, its victims gassing up to the surface
out in the bay. Yet even smoking on the beach
where the creek dies, feeding the lake,
we served those bells. And returned.

Last Bungalow Before the Ravine

Cradling it, fallen and wet, I cycle one-handed
to the bird lady's house.

                Go around, she says.
A chirrupy pong radiates from cages
as she coaxes the hatchling, flanges heavy as dumbbells,
to open its purple gaping mouth. But the mealworm
tumbles to the side, and each missed waterdrop
strikes a hammer-blow to its cartoonish head.
Its beak closes, slow as a door after great decisions.

Something sidles in shadow along a perch
behind her, as if it knows her thoughts. She sighs,
pulls on a metal glove like a gardener going to war
and slips the chick between bars. A sickled beak
glints in the morning light – snatches the chick
midair, a coin purse – and guzzles it heavenward,
neck muscles rippling under feathers. It blinks.
The bulge in its throat slides, then disappears.

                Next time let it die, she says.
I walk my bike home.

                In the mirror of the lake,
a giant pillow smothers my face.

Photograph of My Parents

They canoe away, my mother's paddle
raised mid-air, unwieldy, my father's
steering beneath the surface. Evergreens
shoot up the shore, late light on their hands
and the eddies their paddles make. We've just
had dinner, and I've followed them to the water
with my rainbow-strapped camera, tripping
my way forward, trying to lead my own life.

They skirt the green darkness that pulls me.
Scant stories of their younger selves. They never
count the ways they love, or choices forgotten
in the family noise. Yet seeing their frail vessel,
I understand their medium. What began as distance
finally arrives. The quiet splash that travels.

Mulmur Spring

In the next room my wife plays a concertina
while our daughter reads comics aloud.
Another lopsided war has started, this one
in Ukraine. The women and children
kiss their loved ones, get on the buses.
No one we know has any control. I stare
through the bent glass, cedar and snow
defying the wind. A masked, tawny dog
sighs deeply in a window seat, listening
for coyotes trotting out of the trees at dusk
asserting with ghostly howls the land is theirs.
A circling, yellow swarm bores into whiteness
colouring the fields with streaks of icy mauve
that glower and dive into the sandy gullies.

These days begin with buzzing, a slow
single fly caroms between rooms, trying to get out.
Coffee, smoke from the wood stove, dialogues
with toys. The raven has a croak foreign to me
that says I must leave here soon, and a little vase
of twigs and black berries, dry husks really,
fills the narrow window overlooking dunes
that once were actively farmed. Now wild hay
pokes through the mat of frozen drifts, forming
a link in me with dozens of little bodies
stuck to flypaper, upside down on the sill. One moves
its limbs as if to flee the salty wetness of my breath.

The dog's head rises sharply. It licks its chops
and stands at attention. The keening begins outside.
My host takes death for a walk, leaving me to scratch
and re-hear halting Greensleeves on the concertina.
Soon she will enter the room and smile and run
her fingers through my hair on her way to the fridge
where a gin and tonic to match mine awaits.
Into the dunes, man and dog disappear slowly.
The empty glass on the table beside me beckons
and I can't say the buzzing prospect doesn't excite,
sinking deeper into the sad pleasure of my feelings.
Coy, make-believe voices float on the air.
A hawk leaves its post, floats broad-winged
over woods, eyes piercing the branching clutter,
its sharp spirit buoyed by the long afternoons.

The coyotes howl again. The door blows open
and new animal spirits arrive, winding upward,
all the forms of human pity licking my hand.
They speak, unobserved, beyond imagination.

Twilight with Waterfowl and Rip Van Winkle

It's here. That moment when the day pretends
it never ends. *Who you gonna believe?* it asks.
Forget that fingernail of moon. No one
is limping across the lawn. No one kicked
the little blue chairs across the playroom,
or pulled you by the scalp onto tippytoes.
And when the sisters pay a visit, the bared
teeth won't sheath or the thunder stop.

Yet spying the weakness in what is close
we often miss the clunky reasons for love.
The geese are waddling up the slope, bringing
their young to the tender fescue under the oak.
If I drank the Kool-Aid, once, and slept decades,
now my lids have cracked. I am still yours.

THE THINKER

Whereas most life, miraculous in its own right, is tethered to the immediate, we can step outside of time... From our lonely corner of the cosmos we [can] touch the very limits of outer and inner space, determining fundamental laws that govern how stars shine and light travels, how time elapses and space expands [and] peer back to the briefest moment after the universe began, and then shift our gaze and contemplate its end.

– Brian Greene, *Until the End of Time*

The Thinker

1. Singularity/Genesis

One must be one with it, the universe.
Its web of threaded variation making
more threads, multiplying. Arrival of waves
on windy land. Sole unhappy islands.
Mathematics of a heron's wing.
River-meander in constant ratio
in H_2O or liquid methane, same
pattern on Earth, Mars, and Titan.
Slighter gravity: no us, no here.
If light were slower, no carbon. Faster,
no oxygen. Survive? Ours is it.
Other flipped-for existences do not.
These our creation stories. Talking animals.
Parables of feather and bowling ball
falling as equals – not falling at all.
Chance flapped into the new night, dreaming.
Triggered a fence-like matrix. And
nothing began, and everything. Then light.
Long before our dusty dog of a world
trotted down steps under a cherry tree.
Three lemons, the vaunted singularity.
Hammering heat, matter's hissing sword.
Sculpted bonsai, quiet, moonlit yards.
The master maker stoking an open furnace.
One must be one with it. The universe.

Egg-like, the sun delivers ancient light.
Downward the energy flows, each step weaker,
a subtle removal of all that is useful.
Cyanobacteria capture photons, off-
gassing oxygen, shaping an atmosphere.
Flagella spin their seeds into webs and ferns.
Australopithecus afarensis hop-walks by,
carrying its peaceful, long-limbed name.
From breast to hands a crying child is passed.
Downward the energy flows, each step weaker.
Fields grow corn, the goats are slaughtered, scribes
watch the sun set, note how many goats, how
much corn, how much water, how much gold.
When almost nothing remains, story begins,
racing over receding waters, stepping
first backward to caves and priestly dwellings,
looking for answers in the land of the dead.
Downward the energy flows, a subtle removal.
The warrior camouflaged for war slides forward
to battle, bright famous day and dark
vengeful night skeins of two plots rampant.
The peacock hops down from the low branch, picks
its way through mudded streets. Tap of the herder's
stick, muted clank of sheep at dawn.
Soon after in the school for Brahmins, chanting
begins, the mythic Vedas memorized
in an unknown language inspired by birds.
A figure, cross-legged in a room, hearing
these things, starts to dwell on what they mean.

iii. Unity/Division

Silence, finally. Baby watches mother,
steps unbalanced across the small gap
in protest, wanting none other, wanting more.
The womb, a microclimate of increase.
Senses begin to function, months in the mouth
riding neurons that never stop competing.
The home, a microclimate of belief
where sounds become ghosts that drag their chains,
and princely taste charms us with betrayal.
Eyes see many fathers: they wobble
and focus. The vent throbs hotly underfoot.
Programmed for impatience, something wants us
to move apart, far from all others
but one, to make more, cast a spell on nothing.
Figures of flat girls in procession
unstick themselves like decals from the bas relief,
tribal lines blandly tramping forth,
mycelia beneath a fat depression.
The obelisk stands, phallus atop the moor,
the rifts as yet imagined, untravelled, no
neutrons of hate, protons of forgiveness.
A house rises. A house, abandoned, falls.
Donkeyed in soft blankets, eyes wide beneath
cold stars, the couple with child keep moving,
bereft, alive with suffering and twinness.

Beyond the high hills, past the grey, stacked rocks,
a tower rises in the plain. A tower
heavy with cannon and mission, a dank,
verminous place of salted beef, smithies
and tapestries, where the priests bend in prayer
and swing their lamps, filling the smoky air
with brute civilization. Rock beats scissors.
The tower is yours. Arrows beat rock. Now
it is mine. But cannon beats arrows every time,
cuts through bodies like tofu, rending
arms, legs, faces, skin. Indistinguishable.
The chanting lasts five days. Five days of slow
procession and hoisted relics, flags snapping
their warring fabrics. A flowering sundial, shadow
cast within the tower's courtyard interior,
betrays the clerics' ancient cult of earth.
They chant for those whom death unites,
to expiate the latest wave of moral failure
whose cause is never found in lukewarm mouths
of bats or pigs, but deep-seated in us,
and must be paid in blood. For the high-minded,
whose blood and when remains a mere abstraction.
For the vulnerable and foreign-tongued, it means
yours and mine, right here, right now. Five days
of clubs and bells and skulls and iron balls.
Then the healing can begin. During the feast,
the tower's long-shanked tables and chilly halls
greet their newest owners – ones more exotic
or less, depending upon who's eating.
Beyond these walls, through the arrow slits,
bouncing tumbleweeds spin their dry wit.

v. *Objects/Distance*

As if to trace the exact curve of the bison's leg,
the animal spirit its body would gladly
give up, for the pleasure of being known.
The magus stares, sketches mountains and valleys
on the moon, Venus as naked slivers. Here
on Earth, the body's scaffold chains you
to slope and shore. The snowy peaks like Nordic
Buddhas observe your heat-loss, your pain, your short-
lived strength for carrying on. Inside their flanks,
deer fat, saliva, ochre and blood – the spat
outlines of a hundred hands on cave walls,
welcoming the Ghost of Future Hunts.
High on the wall, hands move on the kitchen
clock, the shift to humdrum, houseplant afternoon.
What future you imagined, false –
what you learned to sing, utterly changed.
Now, no family's orbiting agenda,
no balance of gravity and spinning out.

Nothing has changed, you say, swinging round,
forever undestroyed and destroying. Yet
to break that embrace, the energy required.
Staggering. Yes, we can. Send packing
a thousand obelisks into orange heaven,
we glorified specks of dust and ice, ploughing
through the morning's dark contingencies.
But what did you meet, past the squat planet?
A subtler nothing, the traced-back wonder of origins,
frontiers of knowledge we cannot see or feel.
You have sent the father packing, climbed higher,

out of myth, beyond the world of mothers,
only to look back at earthrise on the Moon
and turn again to crumbled pillars. Only then
did you realize the cosmic joke: we
mean nothing, but we is all we have.

vi. Movement/Contact

Dishes speak to satellites, metal
choirs of angels wait on *Voyager 1*
and 2, kipping past the Kuiper Belt,
tumbling toward the Magellanic Cloud.
Their golden records spin a panner's dream
in many voices: to end our endless duet
with nothing – to balance the equation,
encounter one sentient lifeform or more
among Drake's ten thousand hypotheticals.
Whoever we meet out there, along highways
of dark matter or lonely spots between stars:
may they not do, to us, what we do to ourselves.

The coder breakfasts in Soho: tempeh bacon,
eggs over easy, lavender latte. He smiles
at white-haired friars gripping guitars,
two holy fat Picassos – then turns to his screen,
fine-tuning a blue-skinned, avatar-assassin
with eight red eyes and sexy spider tattoos
for a software venture's online game.
Along the Hudson, hints of a setting: rocks,
tracks, people. Trundle-splash of engines
exit the yellow mist upon its syrupy surface.
The sun leaps into the sky, jarring disorder
back from the pavement, back to shady lanes
and the far shore. Opposite Weehawken,
a rush of steel passes within inches
of the inattentive flaneur, causing him
to jump. He is now of two minds and two worlds,
equally unreal: impact, nonimpact.
An old man coughs. *My name is Ali*, he says,
head bobbing expectantly. The coder cries,
recognizes his own work, whetstone and knife,
the leaping red light of a desert campfire.
He replays his stroll through Sunday's vacuum.
My name is Ali. The coder laughs. Are you
the demon in that speeding car? he asks.
Beneath the man's cheeks, soft bones flash briefly
and chemical tides wash across his skin.
He sighs a dry gust of binary breath.
Accept your death, he whispers, alive.

What is this? Music from a little speaker.
A sharp-eyed woman teaches a child,
singing with raised hands, to beg.
Supper? No supper. Silence sits on its crate
in the market, wearing a jacket of resilience.
This is a dream-day rising, up the scale
of musical dollars and cents, heart pounding
out gold nonsense, do re in remembrance of me,
something scribbled on a notebook page.
This is a breath. This the rhythmic unfreedom
that a feeling body follows. This is a girl,
her ear's contour a funnel, each sound
a ghostly reindeer crossing a plain
into flexing, migrating strings. What is this?
These are hands running up and down the neck
of a harp. This is an artist of interiors,
singing for her bread and butter, a woman
waking from a dream of a three-speed bike
writhing beneath her like an ocelot,
the songbird's fury pecking at her heart.
This is a jail, metal door. This, a shive,
a shiverer. An alley leading nowhere.
Don't ask what the wet matchbox told her.

ix. Galaxies/Dance

Behold her boldly striped veil, her speckled
vermillion eyes, beguiling, spiraling arms.
Yet even as he approaches, she rolls away.
A timeless space in a spaceless time,
his rate of change never varies. She is one hundred
thousand light years distant, a rash of red
ceding fast, echo of two bright thieves,
yellowed outlines, feeling no longer felt,
music of the spheres rocking them deeply.
The unseen burbler marvels, primary colours
soliloquizing light on the night's grainy hem,
sucking down their last photon. Could they know?
All their desire lost in purity's chill.
They, their smells, their half-lit, neutral being,
all declarations and fine emotion, the stain
and spin of any presence, ever, gone.

x. The Restaurant at the End of the Universe

The sun has burned long and the sun is gone.
The lights came up, a red balloon, tickled
the Earth to death. In new bodies on Mars,
our second home, we watched the slow glow
like children peering through an oven's glass door,
the tender brisket bubbling, steaming, charring.
We'd already left, our foresight a kind of ark,
pushed grapheme needles above the clutching air
to carry us to barges floating in space,
a great success to match our greatest shame,
terraforming another world to suit our needs,
subverting its own cold flowering.
But we by it were also changed: the light
gravity spurring elongation, and long
ago, grown godlike to our former selves,
we slipped death and merged our thoughts
as families of sensate probability,
bubbling quarks at once chance and intent,
a dark dew forever about to fall. We watch
The Archer exit the stage, pursued by Bear.
Slow rays glide across the fields of space.
The universe equilibrates. All that is
dimmed and damned by all that is. Curtain.

Nobody

Just a handsome bullshitter. No hero
until that cave where the cyclops sealed us in,
filling the mouth with its grey balls.
  It swung two men's heads against the wall,
stripped and skewered them.
Odysseus raised his mellifluous voice,
   playing sly while it lit the fire –

Gotcha, it said, grabbing into shadows,
popping off the captain's head like a bottle cap
then ate him raw, crunching his fine shoulders
  like the bones of an ortolan.
Who're you, it said, turning its corkscrew eye
on me. *Nobody*, I whispered. *I am nobody.*
  Huh. I'll eat you tomorrow, Nobody.

In the morning, light seething through cracks,
it rolled the stone away
and hurried out the sheep. Odysseus
  lay dead still in a pile of marrowless bones.
When it returned, two more sailors turned to meat.
The smell of Ithaca, roasting, unmanned me then
  and in my fear I saw Tiresias, fondling

his changed parts and featherweight body.
I raised a burning natural poke
from the embers and thrust eyeward.
  Odysseus is dead! the freed sailors cried,
  rowing into deeper waters. *Long live*
Odysseus! That name. Such purpose, such *power*.
  I couldn't let it die.

NOTES

"The Writing on the Wall" – the last line refers to the infamous "Notwithstanding" clause in the Canadian Constitution, used with disturbing frequency to undercut the basic civil rights of citizens.

"Blanche Dubois at Mercy Asylum" – the heroine's life in a New Orleans hospital, after being led away by psychiatrists at the end of *A Streetcar Named Desire.*

"Double Dream of Joni Mitchell" – the epigraph is from Mitchell's song "A Case of You." The opening lines refer to her painting, a self-portrait, which doubles as the album cover of *Clouds.* The 49th parallel separates Canada and the United States.

"Dominion" – "Rightness cannot be inherited…" is taken from T.S. Eliot's "Tradition and the Individual Talent."

"An Old Painting of Charleston Harbor" – Charleston, South Carolina, was a primary slaving port.

"Oakville Revisited" – modelled on "The Tantramar Revisited" by Charles G.D. Roberts.

"The Thinker" – inspired by Wallace Stevens' "The Auroras of Autumn." I am indebted to physicists Brian Greene and Brian Cox, whose sophisticated books and television programs helped me to grasp and weave contemporary scientific knowledge into this long poem.

ACKNOWLEDGEMENTS

My thanks to the editors of literary journals, chapbooks and anthologies in which these poems originally appeared:

Font – "The Writing on the Wall"

Maisonneuve – "Portrait with Stuffed Jackalope," "Meditation on a Puzzle" and "Twilight with Waterfowl and Rip Van Winkle"

Bad Lilies (UK) – "Video of a Cougar, YouTube" and "The Boy's Own Annual, 1879-1967"

The Ampersand – "Double Dream of Joni Mitchell"

Honest Ulsterman (Belfast) – "Dresden"

Water Lines: New Writing from the Eastern Townships of Quebec (anthology) – "Step Up, Step Up"

yolk. – "Dominion," "Yearlings" and "King Canute"

The New Quarterly – "My Higher Self" (now in "Dominion")

Blackbox Manifold (UK) – "An Old Painting of Charleston Harbor" and "Study of a Dying Tree"

Canadian Literature – "Night Thought"

Grain – "Piggery Road" and "Photograph of My Parents"

Train: a poetry journal – "Birdstrike"

The Walrus – "Ravens"

Event – "Teenagers" and "Apartment Block"

The Nelligan Review – "Tannery Hill" and "Oakville Revisited"

Columba – "Fletcher's Field" and "In the Country"

Voices of Quebec/Les voix du Québec (chapbook) – "Marina"

FreeFall – "Walter Benjamin in Moscow"

The Trinity Review – "Private-School Survey"

Stand (UK) – "Last Bungalow Before the Ravine"

Dalhousie Review – "Mulmur Spring"

"Double Dream of Joni Mitchell" was commissioned for the Blue Metropolis project *Life as a Song* and performed live at Le Lion d'Or, Montreal, October 21, 2021. Hearty thanks to Linda Amyot and Sylvain Massé. Early versions of "Dominion" and "National Animal" appear in the anthology *Resisting Canada*, edited by Nyla Matuk. "The Thinker" appears as a chapbook published by James Hawes at Turret House Press.

Grateful thanks to my fine editor Carmine Starnino; to James Arthur and Jeffrey Levine, who read earlier versions of this manuscript and made many excellent suggestions; to Ayaz Pirani for his inspired reordering of poems; to Karen Solie and members of her 2023 Uncertainty workshop for their helpful comments on "Video of a Cougar, YouTube"; to Josh Mehigan's Versification workshop for the assignment that led to "Ghost Bike"; to Sue MacLeod for the workshop exercise that inspired "Dominion," and to Ennie Gloom for suggesting a new ending; to James Pollock, who helped bring the idea behind "Nobody" out of the cave of my mind and onto the page; to early readers Stephanie Bolster, Heidi Lynn Nilsson, Sean Singer, Nyla Matuk, Darren Bifford and Jeramy Dodds; to the Elizabeth Bishop House in Great Village, Nova Scotia, and manager Laurie Gunn, for providing me time and space to work on this manuscript; to the Abbey at Saint-Benoît-du-Lac, Quebec, for same; to Diane Seuss, Annick MacAskill and Jim Johnstone for carefully reading and saying nice things about these poems; to David Drummond for his fantastic cover; and above all to my wife Saleema, my first reader and love of my life, for her patience and wise counsel.

Finally, many thanks to my publisher Simon Dardick and everyone at Véhicule Press.

Talya Rubin • Richard Sanger • Stephen Scobie
Peter Dale Scott • Deena Kara Shaffer
Carmine Starnino • Andrew Steinmetz • David Solway
Ricardo Sternberg • Shannon Stewart
Philip Stratford, trans. • Matthew Sweeney
Harry Thurston • Rhea Tregebov • Peter Van Toorn
Patrick Warner • Derek Webster • Anne Wilkinson
Donald Winkler, trans. • Shoshanna Wingate
Christopher Wiseman • Catriona Wright
Terence Young